Psalms

OF A
LAYWOMAN

Edwina Gateley

Foreword by Richard Rohr, O.F.M.

A SHEED & WARD BOOK

ROWMAN & LITTLEFIELD PUBLISHERS, INC.
Lanham • Boulder • New York • Toronto • Plymouth, UK

A SHEED & WARD BOOK

ROWMAN & LITTLEFIELD PUBLISHERS, INC.

Published in the United States of America
by Rowman & Littlefield Publishers, Inc.
A wholly owned subsidary of The Rowman & Littlefield
Publishing Group, Inc.
4501 Forbes Boulevard, Suite 200
Lanham, Maryland 20706
www.rowmanlittlefield.com

Estover Road
Plymouth PL6 7PY
United Kingdom

Printed in the United States of America

Cover and interior design: Biner Design
Cover art used with permission from Christie's Images/
SuperStock

Library of Congress Cataloging-in-Publication Data
Gateley, Edwina.
    Psalms of a laywoman / Edwina Gateley ; foreword
by Richard Rohr.
        p.   cm.
    Poems.
    ISBN 1-58051-052-3
    1. Christian poetry, American. I. Title.
PS3557.A859P35   1998
811'.54—dc21   98-37741
                                                                    CIP

*For Maureen
and for all
the women and men of the
Volunteer Missionary Movement
who serve God's people
throughout the world*

Contents

Foreword

THE PSALMS always seemed like lovely poetry, wonderful cheerleading for the power of God, striking metaphors. For me, the Psalms have also meant years of mandated Gregorian chant and profound body bows—that is, until I found myself in dark nights of faith and fear. Only then did they become for me what I think they always have been: prayer—as good as it gets!

Although immediate images are often Jewish and, one would think, culturally specific, the Psalms could be written (for the most part) by a contemporary seeker who is in love with the earth, in touch with universal virtues, passionate about justice and truth, and swirling in a cosmos of meaning and purpose. Thus, the Psalms can be enjoyed by the educated and the uneducated alike, by Jew and Gentile, by female and male, by anyone who is still hoping for an enchanted universe.

Great religion is also great and healing cosmology. Great prayer forms situate us inside a world that is mysterious and yet benevolent—and inside of a God who is safe and can always be trusted. How sad that we live in a time when

Psalms of a Laywoman

religion is punitive and threatening, and God looks amazingly like an account manager. We might have sung the Psalms well, but they have yet to sing us. Perhaps human experience is still growing up to its measure of Divine experience. The God of the Psalms is, if nothing else, magnanimous and beyond human predictability or temple control. That won't make the God of the Psalms—or people of the Psalms—too popular. Especially wherever God is organized and domesticated into formulas.

Maybe we are just getting ready for the Psalms. Human consciousness as a whole is still a collective teenager, I am told. We are about to turn twenty as we approach the millennium. Edwina Gateley's psalms prepare us for an adult relationship and an adult love affair with a very exciting partner—and a very real world. But be careful! Adult relationships are filled with too much truth and too much reality for most of us. Who wants to bear that much mystery, that much unresolvable tension, that much of God? It would be a lot easier to just go to church on Sundays.

In our teenage years we seemed content with largely clerical, monastic, and male readings of the Psalms. Nothing wrong with that, even if it might keep us isolated in a small part of God's magnanimity. But, we must admit, it was rather

Foreword

limited and in some ways utterly inadequate. The Psalms do not appear to be clerical, monastic, or male songs at all, but the songs, prayers, and laments of very ordinary people who have fallen into the hands of the living God.

Here, on the eve of the third millennium, a wonderful advancement is taking place: we are learning to see life through eyes other than those of the privileged and educated few. At last we are reading and trusting reality through the experience of woman, through the outcast perspective of the poor, through the non-dualistic minds of native and Asian people, through the sometimes clearer seeing of "sinners," and even through the eyes of—a laywoman! This is a major advancement in human consciousness. I think we are ready to turn 20!

Thank you, Edwina, for giving us these gifts of word and prayer and hard-won faith. We are learning to be worthy of them.

Richard Rohr
Center for Action and Contemplation
Albuquerque, New Mexico

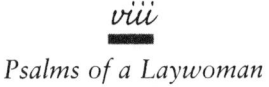

viii

Psalms of a Laywoman

Introduction

PEOPLE ALWAYS TOLD ME there was little market for religious poetry. It was with some trepidation, therefore, that the first edition of *Psalms of a Laywoman* was published in 1981. The response and the complete sellout of the first edition, however, convinced me that people are hungry for personal and authentic "God-experiences." I believe all of us are blessed with these experiences and that our lives are popping with miracles and revelations. The problem is we do not discern or recognize them.

In this book I have tried to share my experiences of God. Many are painful and shot with struggles and loneliness. (God's absence is as powerful as God's grace.) They are authentic expressions of my personal experience in my search for God. I have recorded both joys and sorrows in this search, I have shared my darkness and my light. That in itself is a risk. But I believe it is a risk worth taking if it leads others to become more aware and confident of their own experiences of God and their own potential to seek and embrace the living Spirit within them.

ix

I offer here a brief historical review of the Volunteer Missionary Movement, out of which these psalms took shape. With this brief history as a backdrop, I hope my book gives testimony to God's action in the world today and God's call to all of us to become fully and actively involved in calling forth the Kindom throughout the earth.

The Origins of a Lay Missionary Movement

I was born in a small village near Lancaster, England, in 1943, and was a child during the war years. I still recall the great care my mother took in counting out the ration coupons for sugar, tea, and various basic food-stuffs. We were a fairly poor, working-class family, and I was a middle child—flanked by an elder brother and a younger sister. Both were, I felt, better looking and more intelligent than I. So I began to cultivate a competitive spirit from a rather early age. However, I did not have much confidence in myself and failed to gain entry into the "better" schools to which my brother and sister went. In spite of this, I was determined to do well at school.

During these early years, God broke through into my life in a powerful way, and I was very much aware of being "called" to some kind of service in the Church. As a child, I experienced the joy and surprise of being called by God, which I describe in the psalm "Memories." This sense of being called left me with a longing to love and serve this God all my life. At the age of fifteen I decided I would be a missionary.

"Helping" the Missions

In 1964, at the age of 21 and armed with a degree in teaching, I went off to Africa to work in a mission school in Uganda. Because I was simply a "volunteer" helping out, I was not considered an intrinsic and full member of the missionary activity of the Church. Although it was a rich and exciting experience, I soon realized that it was not my calling to work within a religious structure in which I did not quite fit.

On My Own: School in the Village

After a year, I launched out on my own to set up a school in the small African

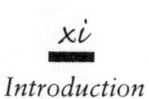

xi

village of Kyamaganda, eighteen miles from the nearest town. I had over sixty children between the ages of eleven and eighteen. Facilities were poor and equipment minimal. There was no electricity or running water, and the main diet was steamed banana with peanut sauce. Life was definitely very simple! But I loved the people and began to learn their language and their ways.

My experience in the village taught me that mission was not all I thought it to be; it was not a matter of my going off (I, Edwina, a Western Christian) to some developing country to convert and teach "the poor." Rather, it was a mutual exchange and sharing of faith, gifts, and culture. The Ugandan people taught me many things. I was in awe at their hospitality, generosity, patience, and extraordinary ability to live fully in the present moment. All this gave me a new and revitalized experience of God, who is found in all peoples and in all religions. This cross-cultural experience influenced and shaped the rest of my life.

During this time, I became increasingly aware of the very real conflicts and problems involved in being a lay missionary without the same credibility and support as the religious and ordained missionaries. As a layperson, I did not quite fit into the missionary Church as it was then. I felt alone and alienated without the

Psalms of a Laywoman

support of a community and with a deep awareness that I was considered somewhat "odd."

But life in Kyamaganda, with all its joys, was hard. Loneliness, poor diet, lack of facilities, and repeated attacks of malaria gradually weakened me and left me, after two years, feeling ill and insecure. Sick and confused, I returned to England in 1967. It was an awful time! I had come to love the people I now had to leave. Yet, I saw no future for myself at home. I had to try and make sense of God's calling about which I was deeply convinced, but which, it seemed to me, had no place in the Church. These deep experiences of isolation and confusion are reflected in some of the psalms.

I began to try to lead a "normal" life, moving into an apartment and pursuing a teaching career in the north of England. But I was restless and disturbed. I could not shake off my deep desire to be a full and active minister in the missionary Church. I knew that deep within, I had a dream and I could never accept anything less than following that dream.

I began to share my dream by advertising in the local newspaper to recruit men and women to go to Africa as volunteers. I was amazed at the response. Within a few months, the advertisements, plus a few talks that I gave to local groups, resulted in over a dozen people eager to

be sent to work in Africa. I was elated! It was all done in a rather clumsy and unprofessional manner as I "interviewed" the candidates at train stations and restaurants and promptly sent them off to Africa in their first wave of enthusiasm. I had made contacts (bishops and missionaries) in a number of countries, and all I did was recruit people with the required qualifications, get airline tickets from the prospective employers, and put volunteers on airplanes!

The whole experiment did not last long. After a few months, problems began to arise, and the volunteers complained of loneliness, malaria, and difficulties in relating with the people. I felt devastated by the fact that these, my first recruits, were meeting problems that they could not cope with and were therefore returning to England. I also felt frustrated and angry because I knew that their needs should be met—and were not being met—by myself and the Church. I began to realize that I was making a mistake—it was simply not right to send people off to another country without proper selection, preparation, or ongoing support. I stopped advertising and wondered what to do next. I was very much aware that there was a real need for lay missionaries in developing countries, and that there were many people in Britain eager to respond to the needs. How could this be done effectively?

A Calling
Becomes Clear

ONE DAY IN JANUARY 1968, I read the Vatican Council documents on "The Apostolate of the Laity" and "The Missionary Activity of the Church." These two documents affirmed my dreams. They expressed the kinds of ideas that had been vaguely going through my mind. They called for laypeople to gather together and organize their own forms of missionary activity under their own leadership, with proper preparation and formation for their members. The Vatican Council documents stressed the ministry of the laity and called on Church leaders to recognize and support such new lay ventures. My enthusiasm and hopes were renewed! The documents confirmed my call to be a catalyst for the emergence of a true lay missionary movement in the Church. But I had no idea how I could go about such a tremendous task.

A retreat was in order, so I booked myself for a five-day retreat to pray, reflect, and decide what to do. The priest-director of the retreat offered to help me by giving me a place to start and all the support I needed to launch a lay missionary movement. It seemed providential, and the offer was too tempting to refuse. I gave up my job and my room and moved to the far north of England to work with the priest to develop the new organization.

It soon became clear, however, that the two of us had distinctly different ideas as to what a lay missionary movement and the spirituality it called for were all about. I believed it was important to challenge the laity to develop their own form of leadership and their own spirituality, and to make their own unique response to mission as lay Christians. I felt this so strongly that I left this newly founded organization when it did not respond to this need. The struggle and the disappointment of my first attempt to establish a lay missionary movement helped clarify my ideas and thoughts. It also helped me understand that any coming to birth involves struggle, and led me to express them in these psalms.

Struggles

Convinced that God was asking me to continue trying, I traveled around the country explaining my vision to anyone who would listen—sisters, laypeople, priests, and bishops. I gave talks, addressed various small groups, and wrote articles for publication. It was a hard time because I had to live on charity, accepting whatever money, food, or hospitality was offered. The

Psalms of a Laywoman

hardest thing was the disbelief I encountered. The vision I saw so clearly was too unreal to some and too threatening to others.

It was also obvious that my first experience of trying to start a lay missionary organization and then leaving it was seen by some as a failure. I was somewhat suspect as being unreliable and unstable. My reputation was not too good!

My efforts, my enthusiasm, and my passionate conviction all seemed to no avail. Why should they believe in me? Why invest money or property in me?

By the end of 1968, I was dispirited and weary and ready to give up the whole dream. But I still had a hope left: John Cardinal Heenan of Westminster. An interview with the cardinal was my last attempt to win support for the foundation of a lay missionary movement. But I was not prepared for the kind of questions the cardinal asked me: "Are you trying to start a religious order? . . . a secular institute? Will you take vows or promises?" I did not want any of these things! I only wanted to share with him my vision of a lay missionary movement, autonomous and free and led by laypeople. At the end of the interview, the cardinal declared that the Church was not ready for the kind of lay missionary movement I envisaged; according to him the idea was premature. I was shattered.

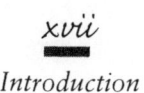

The Foundation of the VMM

Totally disillusioned and wondering why God had treated me so badly, I returned to Uganda in October of 1968. But in December 1968, I received a letter from the Missionary Institute in London saying that they were willing to offer me a grant and a house in London to begin the movement.

At that stage, I was reluctant to return to work in a Church where I had experienced so much struggling and reflection. However, the missionary societies were sincerely reaching out in support. So in January 1969, I returned to England and began advertising and recruiting, drew up an orientation program, and contacted bishops and missionaries throughout Africa. With that, the Volunteer Missionary Movement began. In the next few years, hundreds of men and women were recruited, trained, and sent to work in Africa, Central America, and the Far East.

In Search of Community

As the years passed, I began to feel the pressure of carrying the responsibility of the

whole movement. By 1973, I knew that the VMM needed some kind of continuity in leadership involving more than just one person. I should no longer be alone.

The idea of community emerged. I felt that if I could gather a group of returned missionaries and invite them to live and work together at the heart of the VMM, the movement would be on firmer grounds, and we would have an opportunity to initiate a new expression of Christian community in the Church. I was excited and exhilarated by this new inspiration.

Thus, a small group of us gathered together and discussed the new dream. We began to save money, borrow money, and make appeals for funds as we searched for a house where we could begin community. There was, however, a great deal of scepticism and opposition from those who felt that the VMM should not be expending time, energy, and money on forming community. They saw the VMM only in terms of recruiting and sending out lay missionaries for a couple of years. The idea of anything more permanent, such as a life commitment to mission, was unacceptable.

As opposition from the institutional Church mounted, and my leadership of the VMM was in jeopardy, we were pressed to drop the whole venture of community. But the small group who had gathered was convinced it was right, and we decided to go ahead. So the embryonic community, unsure of its role and future but very much inspired by the Spirit, finally began in January 1975.

We had problems from the very beginning. Within a matter of months, only two of the original six people remained. Feeling like abysmal failures, and somewhat of a laughing stock, we were ready to abandon the whole idea when a priest friend of ours said: "As long as there are two of you, I will believe in you." We were encouraged. We prayed hard for perseverance and invited returned lay missionaries to spend weekends with us to discuss the whole concept of community within the VMM.

LOOKING FOR A HOME

THE NEXT TWO YEARS continued to a time of struggle and bewilderment as the new, young community tried to find and define its role and place in an institution that was still suspect of anything young and new. This experience is reflected in the section of psalms titled "The Struggles." Although we lost our training facilities and were on the edge of bankruptcy, our small group remained utterly convinced that God was calling us to a new expression of mission and community. We held on in faith, and one day a miracle happened: the diocese of Westminster gave us a long-term lease on a thirty-five-bedroom home in Hertfordshire, England, with four acres of land. We rejoiced! As the new community moved in, VMMs and friends came down from various parts of the country to paint, clean, scrub, fix broken windows, clean the overgrown land, and generally make the house habitable.

In November 1977, the first VMM orientation program was held at the new center with the VMM community in residence. The VMM was well and truly launched. Other communities soon formed in Ireland and Scotland, and eventually the United States.

New Steps

By 1979, the VMM was ten years old and had sent over five hundred lay missionaries to work in twenty-six countries throughout the world. It truly was a strong and growing movement with a real sense of purpose and mission, a vigorous Christian community at its head, good formation programs, and an active ministry. Truly God had worked wonders!

I began to feel, however, that it was time for me to move on. I have a deep conviction that we should not hold on to leadership positions *ad*

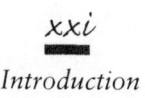

infinitum, but that we should always call forth new forms of leadership from the people of God. The Church, like any institution, is always in need of new life, vision, and renewal, which can only come from openness to the work of the Spirit in other people. I felt I had given the movement as much as I could and that it was time for me to explore new possibilities.

Nevertheless, leaving the movement I had struggled so deeply to give birth to was an extremely difficult step. In the psalms "Letting Go" and "Leaving and Following," I pour out my pain and loss.

FROM THE SAHARA TO CHICAGO

AFTER LEAVING THE VMM community in May 1979, I spent three months in the Sahara Desert. It was a time of solitude and prayer in thanksgiving for all God's blessings, a time of abundant joy and renewal, and a time of deep awareness of God's presence. I express the blessings of this time in the collection of psalms titled "The Desert." It was also a time of listening and of preparation for my next step. In September 1979, I went to Catholic Theological Union in

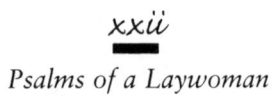

Chicago to begin my studies for a degree in theology. It was in Chicago that my collected psalms were first published. Seven subsequent reprints were sold out—a testimony to the universality of the spiritual journey reflected in this little volume.

The
Psalms

PART ONE

The Call

STIRRINGS

There is a strange,
Untouchable, unseeable
Thing in me.
It hungers,
Grasps, strains
For something
I do not know,
Far beyond—

It stirs,
Turns, disturbs.
It brings with it
Unknown things,
Unidentified longings.
It reveals a vision hazy,
Far, far,
Very far away.

THE NOT YET BORN

Volcano—Volcano.
Bubbling rich red.
Steaming.
Spirit—creation
Bursting. Bursting
For release and life.

And I must
Carry you
Hot and aching
Within me
Until your time
Is come.

Mysterious,
Lonely gestation,
Formed in darkness.
Fed and nurtured
By a life and spirit
Breathing gently, powerfully,
In my soul.
Hush. Silence.

➤

The time is
Not yet.
Now is only
Slow murmurings
And gentle stirrings.
Oh! Not yet born!
But how you live!

I love you, Volcano.
I love your
Sweeping pain
And thrusting, tentative
Movement.

I love you, Volcano,
As you sleep and wait
Within me
For your life.
And for your death.

A Dream
I Have Not Dreamt

There is a dream
I have not dreamt,
A vision
I have not seen.

There is in me
A fearsome longing,
Deep as primordial waters
And rooted in
The very womb
Of earth's fire.

There is in me
A life not become,
Stirring and reaching out
From the dreams and terrors
Of dark history.

➤

There is in me
A fire not kindled,
Glowing like a lone
And passionate sentinel
Awaiting the dawn.

There is a dream
I have not dreamt,
A vision
I have not seen.

RESTLESSNESS

My spirit is restless.
I feel myself straining and grasping
For something
Which has
No form
Nor can be articulated.
I only know
That a power moves within me
And disturbs me in the day
And in the night.
I only know
There is a call
I cannot hear,
A vision
I cannot see,
And the pain I feel
Is inadequacy—
Deafness—
Blindness.

➤

Deaf and blind
I sob,
Alone,
In a pain
That cannot be shared,
A cry
That cannot be heard.
Blank, colorless, formless,
Seeping—saturating.
Strange force
Which defies my grasp
And my control.
And I will cry
Against
This half-death!
This night
Without star!
For I do not want
To die. . . .

INVITATION

In the face of your love I'm a coward to give.
Your demands, your totality, make me afraid,
Weak to respond to such strength and such fire,
Trembling to pursue a love so true.

Desiring, yet dreading, drawn reluctant
To a flame devouring, all consuming,
Taut with resistance against the love
That demands such total giving.

Tempting—the joyless comfort of darkness.
Tempting—the undemanding shadows.
Oh! Let me run and let me hide
From the love which will embrace my all!

Night of indecision, night of pain
Dancing and taunting and laughing before me.
Oh! In the comfort of your shadows—
Let me curl and let me sleep.

CALLED TO SAY YES

We are called to say yes
That the Kindom might break through
To renew and to transform
Our dark and groping world.

We stutter and we stammer
To the lone God who calls
And pleads a New Jerusalem
In the bloodied Sinai Straits.

We are called to say yes
That honeysuckle may twine
And twist its smelling leaves
Over the graves of nuclear arms.

We are called to say yes
That children might play
On the soil of Vietnam where the tanks
Belched blood and death.

We are called to say yes
That black may sing with white
And pledge peace and healing
For the hatred of the past.

We are called to say yes
So that nations might gather
And dance one great movement
For the joy of humankind.

We are called to say yes
So that rich and poor embrace
And become equal in their poverty
Through the silent tears that fall.

We are called to say yes
That the whisper of our God
Might be heard through our sirens
And the screams of our bombs.

➤

We are called to say yes
To a God who still holds fast
To the vision of the Kindom
For a trembling world of pain.

We are called to say yes
To this God who reaches out
And asks us to share
This amazing dream of love.

MEMORIES

It was here, in this great and grey cathedral
That you surprised and captured me—
A child in school tie and blazer
Held awestruck by the vast silence
And cool dampness
Of these pillars and frescoed walls,
Gold angels' wings, set in rows
Against a thousand stars,
Virgins, saints, and martyrs
Clasping lilies and jeweled staffs . . .

And there, hanging before me
By the fourth pew,
The great silent crucifix
Bearing down
And breathing upon me
Its lonely mystery.
Statues solid and secure,
Speaking calm and peace
To my staring eyes
Seeking to catch them out
In movement.

➤

Massive sacred altar for the blessed!
How I loved the ritual and the liturgy.
Its incomprehensible movements and
    language—
Secret cult of which I was a silent part.
And the great grey cathedral
Was mine!
Mine in which to wander and be amazed,
Mine in which to cry and whisper,
Awed by a mighty sense of being.

It was here, in this great grey cathedral
That you surprised and captured me.
It was here, so young, so naive,
And so ready to love,
That you stole from your shadows
Upon me
And clasped me
Your whisper echoing from the great
    stone pillars,
Rushing past the rows of angels' wings
And reaching from the sacred altar.

Yes, it was here,
Here that you broke through your splendid
fortress
And bent to kiss and claim
An amazed and wondering child.

The Call

PART TWO

The Struggles

Abba

Abba, Father,
I love you.
Abba, Mother,
I thank you.
Abba, God,
I am not afraid.
So let me walk
Your way
Wherever it may lead.
Only God—
Go before me.

FEELING ALONE

Sometimes God leaves me alone
Or leaves me to feel
That I am alone.
I wonder what it's all about—
Am I wasting my time—
Are my eager efforts,
Laughable,
Doomed to fall and crumble
On stony ground?
With enthusiasm
And childlike hope,
I step forward—
Hands outstretched
To grasp the Infinite.
Ungraspable
Intangible
Elusive.

➤

I stand
Disappointed, crushed
With outstretched hands
Falling . . .
Empty.
Abba!
Mother!
God!

DON'T LET ME SAY ENOUGH

Tax me not, my God,
Beyond my strength,
Or the strength,
Cold and impenetrable,
That visionless men
Would armor me with.
O God, this is
A lonely banner
You would have me hold.
How many times has its weight
Gripped me in loneliness and fear?
Will they not see, O God,
Beyond the banner?
Will they not see, O God,
Beyond the power and the glory?
Will they not see, O God,
Beyond the laughter and the charm?
O God! Will they see
Nothing more!

➤

I am weary, God,
Of tears and anguish in solitude.
I am weary, God,
Of the visionless men.
I am weary, God,
Of the empty glory and acclaim
Churned out unthinkingly
Without understanding.
I am weary, God,
Of your banner.
Where now is your Spirit in me?
(O God—hold out your hand!
Take this from me
Or hold it firm with me.)
Where now,
Your joy and peace?

Enough, again?
Must I say Enough?
Don't let me say Enough!

DOUBTS

O God, that I may see a little,
That though I seem confident and
    sure,
I be aware that I also can be wrong,
That I might never be so sure of
    myself
That all doubt is swept aside.
For I am human and should be
    prepared
To be brought low,
To be found mistaken.
O God,
Don't let me claim confidence in you
Where it is only confidence in myself.
Don't let me seek a new way
Only because it challenges me
But may not be right for others.

➤

Give me, God,
The wisdom to see
What you will
And not what I want;
What you have planned
And not what I have dreamed;
What you wish to build
And not what I want to achieve;
The wisdom, O God,
To see the difference,
The courage and humility to accept—
If I am wrong.

Holding On

Has the time come, then,
That alone now and quiet,
The very silence of my room
Shrieks out and threatens me?
The ground that once
Was firm and strong
Beneath my powerful stride
Shudders and shifts
And shakes my being.
I retreat into my room
Like a fugitive,
There to fall back,
Numbed and tired,
To search for strength,
To face that which
I do not understand.

➤

My God—equally present
In darkness as in light,
Stand by me!
Allow me, yes,
To suffer and be hurt,
But not to be broken
Or destroyed.
Allow me to be bruised,
But not my spirit
To be overcome.

I know of suffering
And I do not fear it.
I only fear my strength
To carry it.
I ask not to escape
From the doubts and the pain,
I ask that I might carry them
With grace,
With hope,
With love.

Psalms of a Laywoman

STAND BY ME

Living God—
Stand by me.
Hold me up.
Be my strength
When I am tired,
My inspiration
When I am empty,
My life
When I am listless.

Living God—
I cannot always
Meet the standard
Expected of me,
Cannot always
Be the personality
I am known for.
God, when I fail,
God, when I stumble—

Stand by me.

THE FOUNDATION

Now the struggle is over,
We have it,
We have succeeded.
What was abstract,
What was theory,
What was a dream,
Now is reality.
We have it in our grasp,
It is here—
Before us.

Why then, why, O God,
This fear,
This hesitance and doubt
Which plays before me
And tempers the strong
    conviction
Which once was mine?

Those who questioned and doubted
Now have trusted me.
They have agreed.
They have put their faith in me.
Here lies my fear,
In fulfilling
Their trust and hope
In me.
O God, it weights so heavy
Upon me.

God, don't leave me.
Let me find your strength
In my doubts.
Let me find again
The faith which inspired me.

Now, O God, it is a reality.
Make my faith real enough
To do the work
Which lies before me.

The Struggles

Silent Presence

I thought that God
Had come to me.
That after the wild delights—
The suffering and the joys,
The pain and the hopelessness
Of the years—
That God
had come to me.
That after adventure and
achievement,
Pain, despair, and death,
God
Had come to me.
Yes—with relief and mild
surprise
I met my God again.

And then I saw,
Oh, fool, I saw!
That God had suffered
The pain and hopelessness,
Had shared the achievements and
    the joys,
That God,
All enveloping,
All compassion,
Had been there in silence
All the time.

The Struggles

PART THREE

The Cries

PRAYER IN THE OFFICE

Where is my solitude now, my God?
Where the peace, the stillness
That I might find you?
Where the silence in which to hear
Your voice, my God?
Is it that I must seek you out
Anonymous,
In the constant stream of callers?
That I must hear your voice
In the telephone calls
And conversations?
Is it that I must look for you
In the endless stream of traffic
Which passes my door?
Where are you, my God,
When I have no solitude
In which to stop,
To turn and look at you
In silent greeting?

GLIMPSING GOD

I catch a glimpse,
Now and then,
Of God.
A swift passing
Sweetness
Which makes light
The hour, the day, the week.
Elusive, inconstant,
Yet never totally absent
From the hurtling days
With their shadows.
I grieve
That such a beautiful
Awareness,
Like an unexpected visitor,
Comes infrequently,
Entertains briefly,
And passes
With a whisper.
Is lost then
In the laughter
And the music
Of the night.

I Am Tired

I am tired, God.
Nearly all day
I have felt tired,
And yet not been able
To stop—
Except, I remember,
For ten minutes
To think of you.
And even then,
I thought of all
But hardly you,
And watched the clock
To see when
I must get up and go again.
I am dizzy with the people,
The notes to remember,
And all the confusion
Of many things
To do and think about.
God—there's so much
To remember!

All afternoon and evening, God,
I had a headache—
But even that, O God,
Did not lead me
To think
Of you.
I snatch each night—
The midnight hour,
The only one that is mine—
To turn to you
Only to tell you, God,
That I am tired.

THIS MOMENT

Snatch now a stolen moment
From the hurtling days that,
Undistinguished by their sameness,
Pass without a murmur or a mark.

Make something of this moment,
Let it live through awareness
That its pulse will beat still
When the day itself is dead.

Rejoice in this moment!
Steal away in glee to a secret
    corner
Like a thief rewarded.
This moment is mine—
    mine all alone.

SLEEPLESSNESS

Awake again—at the wrong time,
  God.
And I thought I was so tired tonight,
I thought I would drop off so easily.
Instead of that, completely unexpected
And uncalled for—
My mind is suddenly filled
With thoughts, ideas, plans.
They crop up, keep me alert,
Weary me with their persistence.
And in the morning, dear God,
I'll be dog-tired and irritable.
Will you be with me then, my God?
Will I remember then that I lay here
And thought of you
And turned to you
In my sleeplessness?
Will I think of you again
In my weariness
Tomorrow?

THE DYING

You didn't tell me how bad it was.
You didn't tell me that I nearly died.
Amidst all the work, the fury,
	the haste,
With all the excitement, the plans,
	the hopes—
I nearly died
A death not known, not believed in—
That would have been the horror of it.
Nothing told me.
No one spoke.
And in my dying that no one saw,
I was applauded.
All was mine—the laughter, the smiles,
The adulation,
Stored and gathered,
They were mine.
Only rarely, my spirit disturbed,
I would be sad and wonder.
And then with dash and scorn
I would dismiss
This weakness!

See my work! See my achievement!
Don't these speak for me?
When so many smiled upon me,
So many admired,
How could I die?
But in the years you disturbed me,
    God;
All were sure, except you.
And no one told me
I was dying.
If you had left me
I would have died—
But not known it.
You would not challenge
Nor intrude,
And nobody told me
I was losing.
I lost, God.
What pity, what desperate love
Drove you, then, to come to me?
What, to disturb me at dawn
And in the darkness?

➤

To awaken me in tears?
To touch me then and haunt me
With your presence?
And, taken by surprise
I was afraid.
I—the one who laughed and won,
Was afraid.
I did not come to you.
You came to me.
What had I done, my God,
That you could not
Let me go?
What had I done, my God,
That you pursued me so?

It was you, God.
It was you
Who told me
I was dying.

New Life

I suffered, and now there is joy.
I was lonely, and now there is comfort.
I was desolate, and now there is
    warmth.
I was empty, and now there is fullness.

The years and months of struggle
    dragged on
And plunged me into dark solitude.
And now, why now,
Do I see the light and feel the warmth?
Is it that my despair reached its depth
And God, in pity, said: Enough?
Where was my soul then,
When my spirit was so dead?
And now there is a relief,
An almost tangible gratitude
That it is over
And a spark of life and love
Is born from nothingness.

➢

This will not last forever.
But thank you, God,
For living again,
For letting me know and feel
Your life and presence in me.
And if this hope should die again,
Let me remember
The years of emptiness
That passed.

Stay now, God,
A little longer.

RELUCTANT WRITER

Do I presume to touch
The divine
And squeeze
From this limping soul
A spark and light
To flame and kindle others?
And dare I reach
Into an abyss
To drag forth
A diamond?
And would I—
Small soul—
Reflect the Infinite
Out of my own
Dark nothingness?
Is my pained cry
An echo—
Drenched in emptiness?
Or is it a tiny,
Tiny whisper
Born of an anguish
Not my own
And straining for birth
That can only come
From darkness
And defeat?

PART FOUR

The Whisperings

SILENT GOD

This is my prayer—
That, though I may not see,
I be aware
Of the Silent God
Who stands by me.
That, though I may not feel,
I be aware
Of the Mighty Love
Which doggedly follows me.
That, though I may not respond,
I be aware
That God—my Silent, Mighty
    God,
Waits each day.
Quietly, hopefully, persistently,
Waits each day
And through each night
For me,
For me—alone.

THE WHISPER

Wakeful hours
Full of silences and murmurings,
Province of the gods.
Spirit hovering,
Calling
To communion.
Silence, sweet,
Sweeps my soul
Into consciousness.
Awake, my soul!
For God calls
And her whisper
Shatters my being.
There is no time,
Only existence
Which is because
God is
And struggles to return
To the Creator Force
Which gave it being.

➤

Life calls life,
Love gently touches,
And love,
Reawakened from
Its darkness
Responds and reaches out
To the Source
Which feeds it.
Awake, my soul!
For God calls
And would meet
And love you
In the darkness
Of these sleeping hours.

EUCHARIST

Kneel like a stone,
Empty, unfeeling,
And murmur:
I love you.
Watch the movements,
Unmoved,
And murmur:
Take my life.
Eyes with no shine
Follow the hands
On the altar,
Watch the Host raised—
Plead for significance.
Heads are all bowed,
Responding to the prayers.
Do they feel, these people?
I love you.
Do you know I'm here?
Unfeeling, unmoved, cold.
Do you know I've come?
Waiting, watching, hoping.
Do you remember me?

➤

I thought I loved you once.
I've come again.
The priest offers our prayers.
Yes—here we are.
I love you.
We are going to share
In the Feast.
We are going to drink
Of the Life-Blood.
Follow mechanically, step by step.

I'm here.
The Sacred Host is eaten.
Empty, unfilled.
I love you.
Do you know, God,
That I'm here?

It's nearly over.
But I haven't finished—
You haven't answered!
Didn't I get through?
But you are within me.
I love you.
Wait . . .

No—it's over.
The Mass is ended . . .
They're all leaving . . .
I love you.
Didn't you hear me say . . . ?
Empty, bewildered, hurt.
Kneeling.
Shattered.

SPIRIT-POWER

Power-moving, creative,
A force without origin or source,
Only a mighty whispering Presence
Heaving the mountains
And splitting the earth.
Blind—we cannot see,
Nor smell, nor touch,
But there is an awakening—
An expectancy,
Threading the soul to the beat
Of heart and pulse
And charged with breath
Divine.
Restless, stirred,
We strain to glimpse
The Infinite
Beating and breathing about us.

But the Power-moving—is creative
Only in our fragmentedness,
Moves the mountain
Because we fall beaten
Before it,
Splits the earth
Because we sob in despair
At our frailty.
Power, moving creative—
Seize!
And let us shudder—
In your sacredness.

THE BELONGING

Presence ever yet around me,
Strength unasked for by my side,
Love unwarranted, before,
    behind me,
God within me, God without.

Held still tightly like a child,
With the freedom of a woman,
Certain, sure and more aware,
God is mine and I am God's.

Seen a Love—total, powerful,
Though the vision is yet half-veiled.
God closer, nearer, breathing,
Claiming me, as I would him.

LET YOUR GOD LOVE YOU

Be silent.
Be still.
Alone.
Empty
Before your God
Say nothing.
Ask nothing.
Be silent.
Be still.
Let your God
Look upon you.
That is all.
God knows.
God understands.
God loves you
With an enormous love,
And only wants
To look upon you
With that love.
Quiet.
Still.
Be.

Let your God—
Love you.

PART FIVE

The Stories

THE SHARING

We told our stories—
That's all.
We sat and listened
To each other
And heard the journeys
Of each soul.
We sat in silence,
Entering each one's pain
And sharing each one's joy.
We heard love's longing
And the lonely reachings-out
For love and affirmation.
We heard of dreams
Shattered
And visions fled.
Of hopes and laughter
Turned stale and dark.
We felt the pain
Of isolation
And the bitterness
Of death.

But in each brave
And lonely story
God's gentle life
Broke through
And we heard music
In the darkness
And smelled flowers
In the void.
We felt the budding
Of creation
In the searchings
Of each soul,
And discerned the beauty
Of God's hand
In each muddy, twisted path.

And God's voice sang
In each story.
God's life sprang
From each death.

➤

Our sharing became
One story
Of a simple lonely search
For life and hope
And oneness
In a world which sobs
For love.
And we knew
That in our sharing
God's voice
With mighty breath
Was saying
Love each other
And take each other's hand.
For you are one
Though many
And in each of you
I live.
So listen to my story
And share my pain
And death.
Oh, listen to my story
And rise and live
With me.

Psalms of a Laywoman

THE BURIAL

They buried a monk today.
Uneventfully, simply,
They laid his body in the ground,
Wrapped in a cowl and shroud.
But the earth trembled.

I did not know the man,
He was only a name.
But the bells rang deep
And full of grandeur.
And the earth trembled.

The abbey was cool
And the mighty stones
Spoke the voice of timelessness,
And in their great stillness,
The earth trembled.

The monk had been a soldier,
The dry desert
Had gulped his sweat,
And beneath his clumsy army boots,
The earth had trembled.

➤

The Stories

He had cried alone in the desert,
Seeing his silent God
Amongst the tanks and the guns
And the emptiness.
And the earth trembled.

They buried a man of God today
Who had found life in desolation
And joy in death.
They buried a monk today.
And the earth trembled.

CALLED TO BECOME

You are called to become
A perfect creation.
No one is called to become
Who you are called to be.
It does not matter
How short or tall
Or thickset or slow
You may be.
It does not matter
Whether you sparkle with life
Or are silent as a still pool,
Whether you sing your song aloud
Or weep alone in darkness.
It does not matter
Whether you feel loved and admired
Or unloved and alone,
For you are called to become
A perfect creation.
No one's shadow
Should cloud your becoming.
No one's light
Should dispel your spark.

➤

For God delights in you,
Jealously looks upon you,
and encourages with gentle joy
Every movement of the Spirit
Within you.

Unique and loved you stand,
Beautiful or stunted in your growth,
But never without hope and life.
For you are called to become
A perfect creation.
This becoming may be
Gentle or harsh,
Subtle or violent,
But it never ceases,
Never pauses or hesitates,
Only is—
Creative force—
Calling you
Calling you to become
A perfect creation.

Psalms of a Laywoman

RESURRECTION

Part I

We were fishermen, simple people
Who only asked for a decent living
And a fair deal.
But life was rough;
We never caught enough fish
And our meager income
Was heavily taxed
By the Romans.
We hated them—
Oppressors that they were.
But then one day
This guy came along—
A strange fellow
By the name of Jesus.
There was something about him,
Magnetic, I suppose.
Anyway, he knew how to speak
And how to work wonders.
The crowd loved him,
Followed him everywhere, they did.

➤

We were flattered that he chose us
To be his friends and followers.
We could hardly wait for the Kingdom!
We were sure it was about to come
And we little people would be free,
No longer oppressed and beaten down.
Oh, no, we would have the power then!
Jesus filled us with hope
For liberation.
So we believed in him,
Trusted him,
Followed him,
Proud and flattered and excited.

But then, you see,
Our hopes were shattered.
For our hero—
Our hero—
Well . . . they did him in.
He died upon a cross.
It was so awful. So embarrassing.
We were ashamed to see our hero
Beaten and destroyed.

Oh, what a letdown!
We ran, like rabbits, here and there,
Bewailing our misery,
Humiliated by our pain and betrayal.
He betrayed us, you see,
That was obvious.
Got us all excited.
Gave us great hopes.
Then smashed them all in—
And us at the same time.
He was never very clear, of course.
We never really could figure him out.
A funny guy.
He never minced his words
When he knew things were wrong
And shouldn't be.
He was always putting his foot in it,
Lashing out at injustice and oppression.
He wasn't scared to say what he thought.
But we like him.
And he loved us.
We believed that
In spite of his odd ways

➤

And embarrassing behavior,
He'd win in the end.
Yes, there was something about him.
Till they did him in.

And then it all fell apart.
What was he all about?
He fooled us.
Such embarrassment.
We were the laughing stock.
All that blood and spit and pain
Didn't fit our notion
Of God and Kingdom and power.
Jesus fooled himself and fooled us, too.
Betrayer and betrayed. Simple fools!
So we hid, scared and humiliated.
Ran like hell, we did.
We'd nothing left.
We abandoned him
Like he'd abandoned us.
We could hardly look each other
In the eye.

But then after it was all over,
And we were just mooching about
And miserable,
Something happened.
It was amazing.
Suddenly he was there!
We saw his Spirit
In the life around.
We heard his voice
In the voice of another.
We felt his touch
In the touch of another.
Our world turned over.
We couldn't understand just then,
We only experienced and believed.

From our pain and misery
Came life! Suddenly surging up
Bubbling and so, so free!
And we said:
Jesus-man-hero was killed
And Jesus-man-hero
Is alive!

➤

And then we knew, we knew
That he was man
Because they killed him.
And we knew, we knew
That he was the Christ
Because God raised him up.
And then we knew, we knew
That he was us
And we were to be him.
His life began to speak anew
As we heard again
What he had preached and taught—
Freedom, justice, love.
All the things people couldn't take,
For they are not what we have built.
We have our own gods.
And so, you see, they killed him.
They had to.
He was a threat. Troublemaker.
Sign of contradiction.
When we saw him again,
It began to make sense

Because we realized
It was just the beginning.
We had to take over then—
Carry on the work he'd started.
What a job! What a path!

Oh, what a crazy God
To go so far
To prove the point.
No glory and no triumph.
Only faith that came
Through pain and death,
Faith in our God—human-God
Who taught us such a lesson—
Such a lesson.
Turned us upside down.
We see now.
The path of Jesus is ours,
That same love and action, once his,
Now ours,
But they'll not like us
Any more than they liked him.

➤

We, too, will be a sign of contradiction
To selfishness and greed.
We, too, a threat
To establishment and peace.
We are all this because we believe.
We believe there is life.
And we believe
Because God raised him up.
We know, you see.

Part II

And what of us?
I cannot speak of us,
I can only speak of me
And say that I, too, have seen
This Jesus whom they killed.
And I, too, have heard
All he preached and lived by.
It was once taught to me
In a classroom as a child,
And I squirmed and played and waited
In boredom for the clock

Psalms of a Laywoman

To strike my freedom.
And when the freedom came,
I ran out to the world
Excited and full of joy.
God was simply a reasonable idea,
Somebody had to create it all—
That was logical enough.
Jesus was a bit of a legend.
But I thought of him, now and then.
Sure—he was a good guy.
But he was dead.
Well, he never really lived
For me, you see.
But they told me I should believe.
So I said I did
And even thought I did.
I prayed to God and Jesus—
That was the right thing to do,
They told me.
But people and life
Were more interesting
Than a benevolent, boring God
And a dead Jesus.

➤

So I leaped into life
And into the world.
Jesus was dead.
And I was alive!

But something happened to me.
I looked and saw pain and despair
In the world
Into which I had leaped
So sure and proud and triumphant.
Reaching out to the pain I cried:
This must not be!
This cannot be!
(But you see, Jesus was dead.)

Then something happened to me.
It was amazing.
Suddenly he was there!
I saw his Spirit
In the life around.
I heard his voice
In the voice of another.
I felt his touch

In the touch of another.
My world turned over,
And I knew, knew without a doubt,
That Jesus was alive,
And I knew that he was the Christ
Because God raised him up
For I had seen him.
From my own pain and my own
    despair
I had seen him,
And in my Yes, though anguished,
Was Yes to all that he had stood for,
Lived for, died for.
The cross, the death—
I saw the reason why,
Foolish, foolish reason.
Amazing.

But I believed, you see,
Because they killed me, too.
I had my death
And God raised me up.
I live now as Christ does.

➤

I live to proclaim
What he proclaimed—
Life in death,
Liberation from the prisons
That we have built.
And I am free,
Because I died
And now I live.
First, first we must die
To really understand,
For if we follow his way
We must die.
There really isn't any other way—
If you're serious
About the Jesus
Who lives.
Because he died, you see.

PART SIX

The Desert

THE HERMITAGE

It is dark in this rough stone hut.
The desert night is silent and utterly still.
There is only a slight hiss from the oil lamp
Which lights this little corner.
Shadows fall on the oil drum—full of water—
By the wooden door,
And a cockroach crouches
Beneath the huge tin trunk
Crammed with blankets,
Sugar, and rice.
My clothes—limp and creased—
Hang from a steel rod
Wedged between the crevices
Of the stone wall.
A blue plastic mug,
A torch,
And a crumpled Kleenex tissue
Are set beside the sleeping bag
For the night.

It is beautiful and lonely here,
Nakedly simple
With only the bare necessities
To live.

There is a kinship between my soul
And these sharp but protective stones
That make this basic shelter—
This refuge—
Comforting and safe.
I share a peace and a oneness
With the oil drum, the tin trunk
And the bits and pieces scattered around—
Insistent symbols
Of human habitation.

We've been set apart
From the everyday action and interplay
Of life.
The city—the town—
And all their feverish movement
Exist now as memories
And we—the oil drum, the tin trunk,
And the bits and pieces—
Are thrown here together
In this corner—this tiny living corner—
In the vast and silent Sahara.

RESTING

The spirit
Which once rebelled—
Fought furiously
And swept all aside
In its determination—
Now sleeps.
The hunger,
Though not satisfied,
Remains gaping hollowly,
Silently, within.
The restless life,
Undisciplined spirit
Which clamored for freedom,
Now is tamed,
Now gently
Lies and hides
In patient waiting.

HOLD ME FIRM

It is hot and clammy,
The night is thick
With the heat,
And in the silence
God is present—
Captures and envelops me,
Like the heat.

Hold me firm,
My God.
Infuse me
With your Spirit.
I have not the strength
Nor the courage
To love as you would have me.
But as you cannot leave me,
So build me up
And use me.
Make of me what,
From time to time,
I dream of

➤

With a sadness great
That I can only dream—
Make me into a lover,
My God.

Show me your Ways
With patience.
Show me your Light,
Half veiled.
Show me your Life
That I might live.
Abba—
Never release
Your hold on me,
Strong, firm, tender,
Though I laugh before you
And am unaware
Of your Beauty
And your Pain.

TEA IN THE DESERT

Wandering, alone, through the desert.
Sun shrieking heat,
Sweat pouring and dripping,
Rocks, barren and hostile,
Sheltering the brave desert flower.
And I—solitary beating heart
In a vast and empty land—
Wandering, wandering,
Seeking a lost
And lonely God.

Beyond the rocks
A smell of goats
Hanging thick and sweet
In the still air.
And there, standing defiant
Against a thousand miles of sand,
A woman
Burnt brown,
Clad in sweeping black
And colored beads.

➤

We walk to meet,
To cross
The centuries and the nations.
Her eyes, black,
Shining a lost and ancient wisdom,
Speaking the naked horrors and
    splendor
Of uncompromising solitude.
Smile. No words.
Shattering the barriers of language.
Hands touch,
Brown and cracked,
White and smooth,
Clasping and joining
A thousand cultures.

Walk together to her home,
A rough and sturdy shelter
Of rocks and goatskins.
Squat on Tuareg rug
Laid out proudly on the sand.
Smile. No words.
Eyes, searching,

Psalms of a Laywoman

Speaking a million unknown words.
Tea. Thick, hot, sweet,
Prepared with love and care
In an old tin kettle
On an open fire.
Sip. Smile gratitude.
Smile. No words.

Woman of the desert.
Woman of the West.
The world brought together.
Peace and harmony established.
Rivalry and hate abolished.
Black and white.
The lion and the lamb.
Smile. No words.
Tuareg woman.
English woman.
Sharing the Kindom
Sipping tea
In the vast and lonely desert
With a found
And living God.

The Desert

JOY

Let the hills and the plains tremble,
Let the silent sky be shattered
With my cry!
Let the hot stones stir
Beneath my feet
And the startled lizard
Lie transfixed—attentive and amazed—
At the sound of my call.
Let the black desert beetle
Scuttle and hide in new-discovered fear!
Let the mountain birds swoop
Into the darkened crevice of the rocks
As my lonely voice
Breaks and shatters the desert's solitude.
Cry—cry—aloud my voice!
Before it let the mountains crumble,
Let the heavy desert heat be swallowed up
In the breath of the child that cries
Aloud to the God of heaven!
Cry, cry my voice!

Conquer and master the dry, lonely desert.
Drink the solitude, absorb the silence,
And look upon your God.

Hush—be still—
Let the voice fall and be swallowed
In the hot white sands.
For God speaks—
The voice of God unfolds
Like a gentle mantle
On the desert plains—
The voice of God
Strokes the mighty mountains,
Embraces—envelops
The child—alone and wandering
On the great plain.
The voice of God
Penetrates the sun-red rocks
And reaches to the roots
Of the brave desert flower.

➤

Then the child—
Mighty crier,
Bows and falls before her God.
And the voice—now a whisper—
Gasps before the Wondrous Presence;
The heavens are silenced,
The vast desert listens—suspended,
The desert creatures hide and crouch
Beneath their rocks.
And the voice—the tiny voice
Of the child
Fades
Before the all-absorbing glory,
And the gentle stroke
Of a mighty, mighty God.

Psalms of a Laywoman

In Solitude

There is a peace here which surely must
   be rare,
For it is very deep—it soaks into the bones.
It steals in with the moon-filled night
And envelops this tiny stone hut—
Gently, silently.
Peace. All sleeps. Enshrouded.
Listen—listen! Silence sleeps.
Even the cockroach crouches unmoving
And the flame in the oil lamp
Is still—
Still.

My spirit stirs with wonder
As God slips—
Almighty Presence—
Into this domain of solitude
And deeply, deeply enters
Every crevice and corner.
Gently, imperceptibly
Holds my soul suspended
In God's mighty silence.

RENDEZVOUS

It was real and it was a dream.
It was a dream and it was real.
The day had been light, gold,
With a glorious sun sweeping its
    warmth
Over the plateau and the hills,
Soaking its timeless heat
Into the very stones.
And I laughed, and my heart
    laughed.
In joy, like a child,
I scrambled up the mountain
To the top—the very top.
". . . Lest you dash your foot
Against a stone . . ."
An adventure—an adventure—
An adventure with my God!
"Look God—see God—
How beautiful!"
At the top I rested on a rock
And laughed
At the glory all around.

The Pinnacles!
The forms—the colors—
The vast, vast spaces!

Hush—be still . . . !
Was it real?
Or was it a dream?
I could no longer laugh.
A great stillness held me,
A mighty arm enfolded me,
Thoughts and dreams fled
And were lost
In the mountain air—
And I?

I too, lost . . .
A great love had caught me,
Held me,
And I was awestruck and
     amazed,

➤

Emptied of all else
But the vibrance of a love
Which consumed even that
    which it filled.
Aware, hardly, that my heart
    beat—
For it waited on God—
Was startled, then hushed
By the total and swift capture,
Afraid to beat
Lest the Great Lover flee!

Glorious, beautiful!
And in the pregnant silence,
The mighty mountains stirred,
Turned,
And looked upon
The Sacred Rendezvous.

UNION

Moon creeping steadily, throwing
    light
On my darkness.
Heavy night, burdening my soul with
    the weight
Of its emptiness.
And I—
Alone before the silent moon,
Startled by the living pain
Its light revealed.

Soul, naked, bereft,
Sobbing in its solitude,
Creeps,
Confused and dismayed,
To the silent house—
Refuge of a silent Lover,
There to crouch and cry—
Wounded.

➤

Moon, pitying, filters through
Its rays,
Falling and playing,
Eliciting no response, no playful finger
To chase its light.
O, curl, curl, child,
Who would die from too much love
And tenderness
Now withdrawn.

No sound, no cry.
Only a soul's anguish
Heaving silently.
Even the moon rays,
Now transfixed,
Reluctant to play and dance
Before such grief.

Startled—startled now!
In thunderous rush
A Mighty Force
Sweeps, suspends, saturates all
In suddenness stunning!

Fall! Fall!
Loved before the Lover!
Fall! Fall!
Wounded before the Wounder!
Fall! Fall!
On, lonely seeker before the
    Sought!
For now, oh, now God comes!
Now in a mighty rush
God sweeps upon me,
A powerful wind
Lifting my swelling soul
To where
I cannot know
And where
I cannot live.

Swift and silent the capture.
Paralyzed.
No movement.
No whisper.
Only a Mighty Sense of Being
Carried into being.

    ➤

The great Wave,
the great Power,
Now suspended,
Holds and soaks my soul
In vibrant, vibrant Life.
Pain beautiful
Holds me
Poised
Lost
Found
In Sacred Union.

Hush, moon!
Hush, silent night!
Lest in your very stillness
You disturb
The rapture
Of this pregnant hour.

HUSH

Hush, hush, my loved one,
That you might hear
My music
In your soul.

Still, still, my loved one,
That you might feel
My life breath
In your veins.

Sleep, sleep, my loved one,
That you might wake
To my touch
Upon your cheek.

Die, die, my loved one,
That you might live
In my Spirit
Deep within.

Come, come, my loved one,
For you must know—
I have waited long
For you . . .

PART SEVEN

The Letting Go

LEAVING AND FOLLOWING

Gently,
My soul quietly,
Undramatically
Is disturbed.
Who, what,
Whispers in my soul?
Will this God of mine
Not forget,
Nor be satisfied?
What more, now,
Does God ask
To intrude upon
My comfort and serenity?
I have given
This, that, and the other.
Will I have no rest
Until this God of mine
Has my soul and life-breath?
But how I treasure,
In silent satisfaction,
My lifestyle
And all its accouterments!
How happily I possess
My home in London,

Decorated so tastefully
And so well.
How I delight
In the comfort and pleasures
And company
I have gathered around me!
What would you
Trade these for,
My God?
Will you continue
To run your finger,
Gently,
Over these smooth waters
Moving around me?
Will you disturb
My tranquility
Longer, my God?
Or will this be
A passing shadow,
Moving mysteriously
Over my soul
And receding
Into nothingness?

The Letting Go

CALLED TO MINISTER

There is an anguish
In action
After having loved
Solitude.

Called to minister,
Called to lead,
And knowing that God
Has enriched me
With these gifts.

And yet—
Deep and dark and hidden
So far, far within me—
Something cries out
For fulfillment,
An insistent, inexplicable
Yearning
For aloneness,
For a vast desert
Where my soul can chart
Its search for God.

Called to minister,
Called to lead,
And yet painfully reminded,
In the last late hours,
That I was most
And deeply happy
Alone and lost
In the desert sands
In search
Of a lonely,
Loving God.

The Letting Go

LETTING GO

It is time to go.
I can smell it,
Breathe it,
Touch it.
And something in me
Trembles.
I cannot cry,
Only sit bewildered,
Brave and helpless,
That it is time.

Time to go.
Time to step out
Of the world
I shaped
And watched become.
Time to let go
Of the status
And the admiration.

Time to go.
To turn my back
On a life that throbs
With my vigor
And a spirit

That soared
Through my tears.

Time to go
From all I am
To all I have
Not yet become.

I cannot cry,
But tremble
At the death
Within me,
And sob—
Tearless—
At the grief
That heaves
My soul.

Time to go.
Lonely,
Brave departure
That stands
Erect and smiling
Whilst my very being
Shudders
In utter nakedness.

The Letting Go

DARKNESS

There is no light in my darkness,
No spark to break through the void
Into which with crushing swiftness
I am cast without chance to protest.
Oh! Once I walked in joy and
    daylight
And laughed at the dawn and the
    night,
Delighting in God's presence and
Skipping in the light of the sun!

But now I fall before the sunlight
And sob at the memory of joy,
The laughter that danced before me
Echoes and mocks me from afar.
Where once I walked with powerful
    stride
I creep and hide in shadows,
And where once I boldly gazed,
Now I shade my eyes in shame.

No strength to cry—to sob: Enough!
Unable, even, to whisper.
No more to reach and find firm hold,
Only empty chasms around me.
No more to stand on ground secure,
All! All is swept away!
And I, a naked child in the night,
Lost, bewildered, alone.

No God now, to hold me up,
No God to strengthen me.
No Spirit to breathe a touch of life
In this night of desolation.
And the deepest, darkest pain of all
Shrieks wildly through my anguish:
The love is gone! The joy is done!
Curl up—and die alone.

The Letting Go

THE FIG TREE

I saw the fig tree blossom afar,
Ripe and rich against the sun.
And, hungering for its delicate taste,
Towards it I did run.

This fruit is mine! This fruit is mine!
See it hanging on the tree!
And heavy burdened though I was,
I hurried to taste and see.

And as I clambered up the hill,
Hands reaching out in hope,
My feet dragged heavy beneath me
And I stumbled on the slope.

I could not leave my pack behind,
My clothes, my food, my drink.
And I held on tightly to them—
Beneath their weight to sink.

Psalms of a Laywoman

I fell in tears of anguish
And sobbed into the ground
As I realized in my misery
It was mud, not fruit, I found.

And in the silence of my pain
I lifted my head to see,
Humbled and empty-handed,
The rich fruit of the tree.

The Letting Go

WAITING GOD

This is a way
Strange and beautiful,
Full of wild hope
And quiet fear
At the inevitability
Of it all.

For God is there
And God will watch,
Tirelessly wait
All my life,
For me, for me
To come.
And the way is there—
Though only dimly comprehended.

But God—this patient God,
Will never
Give up.

Surrender

Into your hands, God,
This solitude.
Into your hands, God,
This emptiness.
Into your hands, God,
This loneliness.
Into your hands—
This all.
Into your hands, O God,
This grief.
Into your hands—
This sleeping fear.

Into your hands, O God—
What is left,
What is left
Of me.

The Letting Go

The Anointing

There were no crowds at my
    ordination;
The church was cold and bare.
There was no bishop to bless and
    consecrate,
No organ music filled the air,
No solemn procession went before me,
No cross nor incense smell.
There were no songs nor incantation,
And no pealing triumphant bell.

But I heard the children laughing
In the stench of the city slums.
And I heard the people sobbing
At the roaring of the guns.
And the stones cried out before me
As the sirens wailed and roared.
And the blood of women and children
In the arid earth was poured.

Psalms of a Laywoman

There were no crowds at my
    ordination;
The church was cold and bare.
But the cries of the people gathered
And the songs of birds filled the air.
The wind blew cold before me,
The mountains rose and split.
The earth, it shuddered and trembled
And a flame eternal was lit.

There were no crowds at my
    ordination;
The church was cold and bare.
But the Spirit breathed oh, so gently
In the free and open air.
She slipped through the walls and the
    barriers,
And from the stones and the earth she
    proclaimed:
Oh, see! My blind, blind people,
See Woman—
Whom I have ordained.

The Letting Go

THE VOLUNTEER MISSIONARY MOVEMENT:

Its Spirit

and

Lifestyle

At a time in the
History of the Church
When passive obedience and
Reception of the sacraments
Was generally accepted
By the laity
As what being church
Was all about,
The VMM emerged as a
New and challenging movement
Calling Christian men and women
To respond to Vatican II's call
For full and active involvement
In the Church's life and mission.

This involvement has a
Double thrust:
To witness to God's action
Through Jesus Christ
In our world today
And to respond to the
Material and human needs of
The poor and oppressed.

We are first called and
Moved by the very Love that
Lives within us:
"The love of Christ overwhelms us . . ."

(2 Cor. 5:14)

We who have received
The gift of faith
Calling us to
Personal conversion and transformation
Are also impelled
To share that love.
We who have received
The love of Christ through
The Spirit
Cannot contain it.
It must reach out to others
Spilling out and
Touching the world in which
We live.
We believe that,
As in the Parable of the Talents,

(Matt. 25:14–30)

The Volunteer Missionary Movement

We have an
Urgent obligation to
Take Christ seriously enough
To share his mission and message
With others.
We are, therefore,
Sharers of the Good News
Through witness and love.
It is only through
The way we live, love, and serve
That we can truly witness to
The Christ who served
And invited us to do likewise.
Only in following his way
Faithfully
Dare we claim the name
Christian.

"If I, the Lord and Master,
have washed your feet,
you should wash each other's feet.
I have given you an example
so that you may copy
what I have done to you."

(John 13:14–15)

The spirit and calling
Of the VMM missionary is,
First and foremost, one of
Love and service in and to the world.
As laypeople we give a
Special witness
To the reality that all
The People of God
Are called to involvement.
In Christ's mission
All are called to serve.
Bishops, builders, and nurses alike
Must work together
Equally
Towards the coming of the Realm of God.
Mission is given
To us all.

We believe that
God calls us
To harmony, unity
And interdependence.
We wish to dissolve
The barriers that divide

The Volunteer Missionary Movement

People and Church and nations.
We stand for oneness in
The body of Christ.

We commit ourselves
To the service of
Our God
To work among all people
Seeking to break down
All forms of injustice and oppression
And all inequalities
Of sex, status,
Color, creed, or nationality.

"And there are no more distinctions
between Jew and Greek,
slave and free,
male and female,
but all of you are one in Christ Jesus."

(Gal. 3:28)

Of its very nature
This mission cannot be
A temporary thing.

Psalms of a Laywoman

It is a total commitment
To the Gospel
And can be nothing less than
A way of life.

We take the Gospel
Seriously.
We must live it.
In giving ourselves
To each other
We will come
To fullness of love and revelation
Promised through Christ.

We follow him with
That same trust and confidence
That he had in God.
For we know that
The Spirit is with us
And will not abandon us.
"I shall ask God
and God will give you
another Advocate
to be with you for ever,

The Volunteer Missionary Movement

that Spirit of truth
whom the world can never receive
since it neither sees
nor knows her;
but you know Her,
because She is with you,
She is in you.
I will not leave you orphans."

(John 14:16–18)

Our mission begins with
Our faith in the Resurrection
Which sends us out
In hope and love
To all the world.

We also wish to remain
As laypersons
Without any vows or promises.
To demonstrate
The ability of all
Men and women to be
Fully committed Christians
Whilst pursuing
Their own lifestyles

Psalms of a Laywoman

And calling in the world.
We do not separate
Our mission as Christians
From our day-to-day life.
We wish, rather,
To ground our own
Personal and spiritual growth
In striving
To become fully human
Within the context of
Our work and service in the world.
We represent a wide variety
Of charisms and lifestyles
And may be distinctive only
By our commitment and openness
To the Spirit of God.

Each VMM missionary
Takes personal responsibility
To seek and pursue
Fullness of Christian faith
In his or her own situation
And lifestyle
And aware of the

The Volunteer Missionary Movement

Support and prayer
Of the whole VMM.
Our task
is to be true Christian witnesses
In the world
With that freedom and flexibility
That invites and embraces all.

We recognize that
We need each other.
We are a community-based movement
That stresses and encourages
The value of living together,
Praying together, and
Working together.
We believe that it is through
Our shared experience
In family and community
That we will truly
Grow together
In Christ.
Whenever possible, therefore,
VMM missionaries
Live together in small groups

Psalms of a Laywoman

Or renew and strengthen each other
Through visits, correspondence, or
Regular shared activities.

And so the VMM missionaries
Say Yes to Christ
And Yes to his mission.
We say Yes to the Church
Of which we are a part,
And we offer to the Church
Our service, our commitment,
And the vision and the vigor
That we bring.

We must be
Men and women whose action
Is motivated and strengthened
Through prayer.
We gather together
To share our worship and prayer,
Recognizing that Christ is
At the center of our lives
And that,
As People of God,

Celebration and worship
Mean sharing and gathering.

Our prayers, as well as being
Shared and public,
Also involve
Personal and silent encounters
With God
For which there can be
No substitute.

We learn to listen,
In all types of prayer,
Not only to the needs
Of our brothers and sisters
In the noise and action
Of today's world,
But also to that silent movement
Of God's action within us.
We bring together in harmony
The voice of the people and
The voice of the Spirit
And we strive
To respond to both.

Psalms of a Laywoman

VMM missionaries
Are listeners.
Our witness will be seen
When God's Spirit
Is so strong within us
That it is visible
In our lives and actions.

Christ was available to all
And reached out
To the poor, the sick, and the rejected.
He was one of them.
His mission is now ours.
Our mission is to be wherever
There is injustice
Of any kind.

"Wherever there are people
in need of food and drink,
clothing, housing, medicine,
employment, education;
wherever people lack the facilities necessary
for living a truly human life
or are afflicted

with serious distress or illness
or suffer exile or imprisonment,
there Christian love
should seek them out
and find them."

(Apostolate of the Laity—Paragraph 8:4)

The majority of our world
Lives in hunger and want,
Deprived of the most basic necessities
To live a decent human life.
Impelled and driven by
The Spirit of Christ
We cannot stand by unresponsive
To the needs
Of our brothers and sisters.
We must share
Ourselves.
They must have the tools
To enable them to develop
And be free.
They need the skills and the expertise
To develop
Their own resources and gifts.

It is not simply a matter
Of handing out money,
Food, or equipment.
It calls
For more than that.
Our response
Is to share who we are
As well as what we have.
We are invited
To be fully and actively involved
In all areas
Of human activity and development,
Education, medicine, agriculture,
Craftwork, and building.
We are the carpenters,
The catechists, the nurses,
The community builders, the doctors,
And the farmers.
These are the skills
With which we have been blessed,
The talents
Which we have received.
We are not to bury them
But to freely share them

The Volunteer Missionary Movement

So that people might live
And be helped to reach
Their full human potential.
It is not a matter
Of charity or good deeds.
It is a basic Christian obligation
To justice.
What we have to offer
Is what we have been freely given.

We live with the people.
We suffer with the people.
We rejoice with the people.
We become part of the people.
Our sharing becomes
A journey we walk together
Towards liberation
And a reaching out together for
Growth and fulfillment.

But we do not impose ourselves
Or our way of doing things.
We are at the service of.
We are the servants.

This means that
We are available
To go wherever we are invited
In the world.
It presupposes an openness
To the needs of others
And a spirit
Of confidence and poverty.

This spirit of poverty
Makes itself available
As fertile ground open
To whatever fruit God
Wishes to plant.
We may never see
The results of our work.
If we truly follow
The way of Christ,
We will find the Cross
As well as the Resurrection.

The Path of Jesus
Which we freely choose to follow
Has no trace

The Volunteer Missionary Movement

Of glory or honor or pomp.
It calls for a confidence and faith
And looks for nothing
Beyond that.

We are aware that
Through our service
We receive far more than
We are ever able to give.
We realize that
We are enriched
By our encounter
With people of other cultures and
 beliefs.
We come to discover
That we, too, are poor in many ways
And need to grow
Through receiving from those
To whom we go.
Our work
Entails human relationship
Working and growing together
To build a more
Humane and loving world

Psalms of a Laywoman

Filled with the Spirit of God
Who sends us.

Our mission is never complete.
It is an ongoing challenge
Calling us to continual growth.

We the People of God,
Do not establish the Realm of God,
We work towards it
In faith and hope.
We see that we are part
Of a Church which
Is a human institution
Struggling to respond
To its mission
And ever in need
Of growth and renewal.
We go
As representatives of our local churches
To share the gifts we have.
We are in solidarity
With the church that sends us
And have a commitment

To return
And share the gifts and riches
Which we have received.
Our task is then
To continue our work as missionaries
In our own home countries.
We have a prophetic task
To help renew and invigorate
Our own church
For we recognize
Our own needs, inadequacies, and hunger.
We see that mission
Is not a one-way process
Coming from a "First World Church,"
And ending with
A "Third World Church,"
But it is a cyclical process
Going from one church
To another church
In continuous, mutual sharing.
This is the dynamic of mission.
It is never static.
It is ever moving,
Ever growing and

Ever calling forth
The gifts and life in the other.
We recognized
The fire and dynamic power
Of the Holy Spirit in mission
Which cannot be contained by
Or monopolized within
Any human institution,
But which is at work
Where She wills.
We see the Spirit at work
In those to whom we go
As well as within ourselves;
We are channels of the Spirit,
Called forth to renew and strengthen
And be renewed and strengthened
In return.
VMM missionaries are open
To this dynamic and free action
Of the Spirit
Who first inspired and called us
To the service of God.

The Volunteer Missionary Movement

VMM missionaries are
Followers of Jesus
Engaged fully
In the mission of the Church
Through active service in the world.

We praise and bless our God
Who calls us to live and to be
In the world
Sharing our mission
Of love and peace
With all men and women
Of every color, race, and belief.

Psalms of a Laywoman